CW01574921

An*dyne
Magazine

Established 2023
by
Katarina Eva Yepez & Veronica Zora Kirin

Vol. 1
November 2023
-

Finnian Burnett

Anodyne Magazine is an arts and literature magazine highlighting the intersectional experiences of the FLINTA* community's global health.

Anodyne Magazine was co-founded by Veronica Zora Kirin and Katarina Eva Yepez in 2023 in the hopes that at least a few more FLINTA* individuals, looking for an outlet reflecting experiences of health, might find comfort in the pages between the covers of this publication.

© Anodyne Magazine 2023
Cover design and layout: Katarina Eva Yepez
Editing and proofreading: Finnian Burnett, Katarina Eva Yepez, and Veronica Zora Kirin

Printing on behalf of the magazine:
IngramSpark

Anodyne Magazine
Erich-Weinert-Straße 78
10439 Berlin

Contact:

editors@anodynemag.com

ISBN
Paperback: ISBN 978-3-00-077421-8
eBook: ISBN 978-3-00-077420-1&

***

After lifetimes of silencing by an unaccommodating system we have had enough. Our voices have been muffled, our needs ignored, misdiagnosed, and misunderstood.

Billions of FLINTA exist, frustrated by patriarchal structures and standards for health.*

It's our time to be heard.

We refuse to accept outdated solutions to contemporary issues.

Anodyne (meaning pain relief) Magazine is a trimesterly periodical offering an opportunity to voice our experiences to the masses. We exist not only for catharsis, but also progress. With the intersectional contributions featured in our magazine, we hope to change the existing health paradigm.

We are listening.
We support you.

\-

Veronica Kirin and Katarina Yepez,
Anodyne Co-Founders

Table of Contents

*Denotes Anodyne's featured contributor.

Find us at...

Web: Anodynemag.com
Instagram: @anodynemag
X (formerly Twitter): @AnodyneMag

Meet Our Co-founders

Lower left and upper right portraits © Oumou Aidara, 2023

Katarina Eva Yepez

Katarina is a Berlin-based artist with a knack for expressing the inticacies of human experience. Her artwork, which can be found under the moniker Katarina Eva, is bold and expressive with an unmissable touch of whimsy. Though she is primarily a painter, she also works in media including photography, scultpture, mixed-media, and writing. You can find out more about Katarina and her art at:

katarinaeva.com

Veronica Zora Kirin

Veronica is an entrprenuer, writer, web-designer, and woman of many hats currently based out of Berlin. Over the years, she has built non-proits, tech companies, and startups.Concurrently with Anodyne, Veronica's startup AsteriskDAO is revolutionizing women's non-reproductive health. For more on Veronica, check out:

veronicakirin.com

Duo portrait © Oumou Aidara, 202

Anodyne was an idea that incubated for a long time. Something that garnered, "Wouldn't that be great?" from Katarina and I for over a year. For me, even longer. A pipe dream, like a beach house or a mountain estate. Something people dream of, but don't actually do.

It took a fellow creative, someone who was equally focused on the realities of FLINTA health, to bring Anodyne to light. Katarina was the missing half that made it all feel possible.*

We're not here to complain. We're here to create visibility, community, and hope. One of our Kickstarter backers said, "I have all these medical experiences which I'd buried because I didn't know how to process them. The existence of Anodyne gives me a way." I feel the same.

They say 'build what you need.' Together with amazing contributors and editors, we've built what we all need. A way to process. The knowledge we're not alone.And a place to share ideas, experiences, and hope. So grab a cozy drink, curl up in your favorite chair, and join us as we explore the dynamics of FLINTA health.*

– Veronica Zora Kirin

Upon moving to Berin in August 2022, I wrote a 4-item checklist on my bedroom mirror. Accomplishments I hoped to achieve by the end of 2023. 3rd on that list: Print first edition periodical. Unbeknownst to me at that time, that checkmark would come to me in the form of Anodyne Magazine.

More than a tick in a box, Anodyne represents the satisfaction of taking action on a project extending beyond myself. With my own health-related concerns coming to a head, Veronica's message "how serious are you about starting that periodical?" started the conversation which became the magazine you see before you now.

Anodyne makes space for compassionate interactions with the challenges the FLINTA community faces with regards to their health, mental and physical. Anodyne is a resource I would have turned to as a reminder that no voice is too soft to be listened to amongst peers determined to hear it, help it, and validate it. I am remarkably proud that our editors, and contributors have joined us in generating visibility for FLINTA* health worldwide.*

– Katarina Eva Yepez

Finnian Burnett

Finnian Burnett is a college instructor of creative writing and composition. They run an online writing academy for FLINTAQ writers for the Golden Crown Literary Society. Finnian also gives workshops on a variety of craft of writing topics, and they will be facilitating at this year's Northwest Narrative Medicine conference. Finnian holds a doctoral degree in English Pedagogy and their passions involve teaching with story, writing the human body, including mental health, and the intersections of identity.

Their work appears in Reflex Press, Ekphrastic Review, Blank Spaces Magazine, WordWorks Magazine, and more. Finn's latest collection, The Clothes Make the Man, was released by Ad Hoc Fiction. A second flash fiction collection, The Price of Cookies, is forthcoming through Off Topic Publishing. When not writing or teaching, Finnian watches too much Star Trek, futilely tries to grow a garden, and takes their geriatric cat for walks in a stroller. Finnian lives in British Columbia with their wife, and Lord Gordo, the cat.

Letter from the Editor

As an outspoken advocate for FLINTA* health, I hear a lot about women's experiences with health and healthcare—conversations about menopause, menstrual cycles, abortions, fatphobia, and gender dysphoria. I personally experience healthcare from several different sides—as a patient with physical and mental disabilities, a person navigating gender identity, and someone recovering from a lifetime of disordered eating. I also experience healthcare as a caregiver, a facilitator with the Northwest Narrative Medicine Conference, and an instructor on writing one's body, health, and mental illness.

Yet even though I came at the submissions for this issue with my own preconceived notions about what I'd find, I was still blown away by how compelling the narratives are. Some touch on living with mental health issues or on medical fatphobia when you seek help for something that has nothing to do with weight. Me too, my friend, I found myself whispering as I read.

Some spoke of racism in healthcare—a woman who intertwined her own story with her mother's, lamenting how little anti-Black attitudes in medicine have evolved over the years. Some offered poems about self-medicating, self-diagnosing, self-advocating. Many of the stories, poems, and creative non-fiction pieces bowled me over. Because I relate to them. Because they strike a chord. Because they focus on FLINTA* health.

Some pieces instigated conversations in our editorial meetings: Is taking care of one's dying father really FLINTA* health-related? But, yes, we decided. Traditionally, caretaking is a feminine role, and these roles frequently fall to us against our wishes. Caretaking takes a toll on the mental and physical health of the caregiver. Many women spend huge chunks of their adult lives taking care of children, only to then turn to taking care of parents… So yes. A story of caring for your dying father belongs here. And yes, a poem about facing your mortality through a mother's death belongs here.

Common themes emerged from several submissions: how out of control we can feel about our health. Not only because of the care we receive from others, but because of the ways our bodies sometimes betray us. We're angry, sometimes, that our bodies don't listen to us. We're tired, too. Tired of being sick, tired of trying to figure things out, tired of taking care of others when we aren't sure exactly how to take care of ourselves.
And also, we're tired of waiting. Waiting to be heard, waiting to be taken seriously. Waiting to be understood. Michelle Rule, in the poem "Streaming" writes:

But I'm a good girl so I just wait
in this space with all the others
like the little ducklings in the creek
crowding around their mother nurse
wondering which way to go next

Sometimes, we're waiting in doctors' offices, in emergency rooms, in our own minds. But if reading this month's submissions has taught me anything, it's that we're not waiting for someone to save us. Many of the submissions touched on the idea of advocating for ourselves, finding ways to control our narratives, to understand the full complexity of our lived experiences in bodies and minds that don't always work the way we want them to. One of the ways we learn to live with something is to write about it. In this issue, our contributors have done just that. They've taken hold of their narratives, moulded them into something that makes sense to them, something that will hopefully resonate with others.
Here, we share with you the voices of FLINTA* people, not to offer salvation, but to showcase the narratives of people who are finding their own. As Leia K. Bradley writes in a poem in this issue, "I don't need a savior, just the story."

My friends. Here are the stories.

-Finnian Burnett | *Guest Editor*

An*dyne
Magazine

Streaming |Michele Rule

Sitting in the emergency room area
called “Streaming”
but it’s not.
It’s dribbling
like the creek near our house in late summer,
the last of the winter’s snowfall long melted,
no rain for months
only heat, every day
sun beating down on the water
evaporated away to some other place
I don’t know where.
I sit with my toes in the slow dribble
wait my turn to have tests
wait my turn to see the doctor
rethink my decision to even come
as I hit the fifth hour of barely any movement.
My toes aren’t even cold
the water is warm like the broth
that Oma made when we didn’t feel well
not too hot to keep our little mouths safe
but warm enough to soothe our stomachs
nourish our tiny bodies back
from fever or stuffy nose.
The dribble has come to a halt.
A beaver in the shape of a doctor
has dammed up the path
with too many questions
and I’m sitting here thinking of broth.
After seven hours of nothing
I just want to go home
and eat pizza and sushi.
But I’m a good girl so I just wait
in this space with all the others
like the little ducklings in the creek
crowding around their mother nurse
wondering which way to go next
peep peep.

It Could Have Been Worse | Amani-Nzinga Jabbar

"Undress, remove everything, even your underwear." The nurse hands me a hospital gown. "Put this on, opened towards the front." She tells me that she will return shortly.

"Will my husband be able to come back?" I ask for the second time.

"I'll have to check with the Doctor." She turns and exits the room.

I look around at the instruments that surround me. There's a table covered with a blue cloth, and on it lies a tool that, to me, looks like a smaller version of what the carpenter used to apply the glue that made the carpet stick to my bedroom floor. It's even got a similar trigger.

I follow directions, removing all my clothing. Taking off my bra, I'm struck by the heaviness of my breasts. They feel burdened and more sensitive than usual. Because they've been prodded and poked at so much lately.

It started with a sharp stabbing sensation that got worse after my runs. Those runs were meant to be de-stressors, meant to offer a reprieve from homeschooling my 5-year-old, keeping my teens focused on their virtual classes, and demoralizing zoom meetings with my own students. They were a moment of fresh air and greenery, a moment when I could try to forget the world wasn't going to hell. They did that, but after a while I couldn't ignore the achiness in my chest.

After one run, I felt around in the shower and discovered the knot. Then another. The one I was worried about resided only a few centimeters from my left nipple.

It was hard, unyielding, like a tiny marble. How had I not noticed it before?

It took over a month to see the OBGYN. In that time, I began rubbing my breasts with a mixture of frankincense and almond essential oils. It was suggested by my friend who is a reiki therapist. "Just love on yourself," she said. "Everything will be ok."

I tried to believe her, tried to believe in a magic cure to stem my rising fear.Yet I found it difficult to remain optimistic. As much as I tried, I thought of other disasters in my life that, as much as I had tried to remain hopeful about, had taken turns for the worst. I thought of losing my home to Hurricane Katrina, the wounds that the storm exposed, the scars still burning over a decade later.

When I finally got to the OGBYN, she wondered at my ability to find something so small, so hidden beneath my body's flesh.

The mammogram showed the lumps clearly. The radiology report described a partially obscured oval lesion appearing 1.9 x 1.7 x 0.8 cm on my right breast. On my left breast, the report noted a complex cystic and solid lesion measuring up to 1.5 x 0.8 x 1.6 cm. There were other words on the report, ones I didn't fully understand and googling them, something I did late into the night, every night, made my heart race and my hands shake.

The hospital near my home was overscheduled and wouldn't be able to conduct the biopsy for months. So I came here to an unfamiliar place and wait, wearing only the thin white gown that barely covers my body, let alone my fears.

A part of me tries to remain hopeful, but I can feel the tension in my muscles, the clench in my jaw. My body prepares to fight another battle. The exhaustion settles into my spirit. Today's biopsy will tell me how bad it could get, even though my late night internet searches have already shown me bad doesn't cover it. Pushing those thoughts out of my mind, I focus instead on what lay directly ahead.

The nurse returns, without my husband. "You can lie back," she instructs. She covers me from the waist down with a cold white sheet. "I'll inject the numbing now. Are you on any blood thinners?" I can only shake my head. She cleans my breasts with a sponge covered in a frigid red liquid.

"Once the numbing kicks in Dr._____ will begin the biopsy."

"Is that a woman? I had requested a female doctor," I manage to squeak out.

The nurse shakes her head. "We don't have any female radiologists on duty today."

The doctor finally enters the room. "I'll be performing

your biopsy today," he says. "You're in your 30s," he says, looking down at my chart. "You look like you're in your 20s."

My breasts, the ones that nursed three children are bare, exposed, and his casual joking seems ill-fitting for the occasion. Yet, I laugh. Why do I laugh? Conditioning. Anxiety. I need my husband to anchor me here and I ask for him again. "He can't enter the sterilized area," the doctor says without a smile.

He begins the procedure, and my self disappears. The doctor and the nurse know each other. They exchange pleasantries. The nurse says her teen daughter had caught covid a few weeks ago, "But it's mild. We wouldn't know it if she hadn't lost her sense of smell." I'm not here, not really. They banter. Laugh. A few moments later, they focus on my breasts. "The lump on the left breast is mobile," the doctor relates to the nurse, who takes notes on the computer.

I am now nothing but a body. The nurse wheels my table around to better position me for the doctor. He wields the caulking gun looking instrument, and I realize that's what he will use to take out tissue from the area near my nipple. I'm not numb enough, as soon as the thought enters my mind, I feel the pain. Searing through one of the most sensitive and private parts of my anatomy. The tears fall and I'm helpless to wipe them away. The doctor and nurse don't notice or perhaps they don't care.

My mother birthed seven children via cesarean section. After two or three c-sections, the risks for complications increase. Yet, the doctors often treated my mother with a combination of coldness and antagonism. They assumed her pregnancies were the result of poor family planning. They couldn't imagine a black woman actually wanted and cared for her seven children or that they had a father in their life. They urged her to get her tubes tied. I remember my mother saying, "One doctor, she was a white woman, tried to get me to tie my tubes while I was woozy from anesthesia. She asked me if I wanted to get my tubes tied just after I had given birth. I was still under anesthesia. She knew I wasn't in my right mind. They had no respect. I was on Medicaid, poor, and black." I had pushed these stories to the back of my mind but they came rushing back as the doctor and nurse mishandled my breasts. I'd considered these stories part of the past but here they were in front of me, taking place on my body.

How had I not taken her warnings to heart? Did I really think our situations were so different? My mother was poor and on government assistance in the 80s and 90s. I have enough money to pay my copays, good insurance, and we're well into the 21st century. Watching the doctor ignore my pain, banter with the nurse, I wonder if they consider me less than human.

There was a time when white doctors performed experimental abdominal surgeries on enslaved black women, often without the use of anesthesia. There was a time when white doctors tested the strength of anesthesia on enslaved children. One of those doctors, Crawford Long, had a hospital bearing his name miles from my home and it wasn't renamed until 2009. For a moment, I wonder if this hospital ever bore the name of someone who had harmed enslaved children, of someone who made a name for himself tormenting black bodies.

After removing the breast tissue to be biopsied, the doctor places small metal clips in my breasts, to mark the site where the tissue was taken. He stitched me up and left. I feel violated, yet I stand and prepare to get dressed, thankful for the ordeal to be over.

"You'll need to leave your gown on," the nurse instructs.

I can't speak. I thought this was over.

"You need to go down the hall to get a mammogram. We need to make sure the biopsy clips were placed in the correct position."

"A mammogram?" I can't imagine getting my breasts, which have just been stitched up, and are already beginning to bruise being squished between those two cold metal plates. I try not to cry. I ache at the thought, consider running away, screaming for my husband, something. "Are you sure?

"This is standard procedure." I follow the nurse down the hall to mammography. The pain of having my breast squeezed between those two metal plates is more intense than I anticipated and I focus on trying not to pass out.

Tears fall from my face as I leave the hospital's doors.

In the waiting room, I collapse into my husband's arms. He takes me home to try to begin healing. Would I have been treated this way if I didn't live in a black body? The question lingers in my mind for the two weeks it takes for me to receive the results.

They're benign lumps, but one is precancerous. The report called them atypical hyperplasia, an overgrowth of abnormal cells. It has to be removed. My body, my black female body will be subjected to another round of abuse, another white male doctor. For a moment, I consider ignoring it, taking my chances, going back to the safety of home remedies and self-love. But I know I'll go back; I know I'll subject myself to the ministration of people who hold all the power. My body needs me, even if my heart rebels. I know I should count my blessings. I guess it could have been worse.

Elective | Laura Mills

The notes are

sparse.

They tell something different
From what went on
that night.

Space
on the page,
A choice.

The choice to
leave bare,

Where emptiness hides

the choices made
for your coming
into this world.

Absence reigns for
Presence.

ES

The initials float out

alien to me,
my body,
my memory.

Elective Surgery.
The choices behind
terminology.

Suggesting options
But this feels involuntary, pressured, a necessity.
A choice
when you have
no choice.

Suggesting deliberation
But this feels frantic, frightening, a precipice.
The blood,
your spiking heart rate,
source and cause unknown.

Suggesting time
But this feels sudden, desperate, an emergency.
No letter in the post confirming procedure date.
No bag packed carefully.
No bodily autonomy, my consultant informs me.

You are here.

I carry that mark. A forever line linking this body with yours.

In Van Gogh's Dining Room. |Tatiana Shpakow

I take my first antidepressant.

I go through the spleen, digging through the heart
of the kitchen, and set the table for the start of
the morning--a winter-wilted sunflower, an ear
steak, a tube of yellow paint, the color of
what my insides should be.

I stop when I realize I've cut
through the rib cage completely,
digging through the back,
emptying a bottle of blue entirely.

This is not my first little death or little life,
each pill the color of ego that ends outside old church-
es,
those daily pallet cleansers of anesthetic benders,
and women I never spoke to but
wrote poetry about.

My brother comes at half past 7 and asks what I do for
the day
when I stay in this yellow-painted house. I tell him I'm
on the
phone to avoid showing bloodshot--I want to tell him
about my newest attempt by talking about
my dead friends, my alive friends, and all
the people I don't know yet. I tell him I'll never meet
anyone again.

Until now, I thought I was bound
to be a different nose, a cauliflower ear, a simple mad-
ness,
but he frowns, hands outstretched in praise like he's
calming
a rabid dog, and offers me green.

In Van Gogh's dining room,
I take my first antidepressant.
For the first time in 20 years,
It's all yellow.

kitchen poem - *a recipe i'd make on my worst days*
|Tatiana Shpakow

½ cup of whipping cream
I miss the intimacy of those old kitchen poems, love
stored in pockmarked pits and honeysuckle
kisses, cayenne freckles and sweet-sticky
rind crowns, when the sun was just an orange, and we
were friends with our recipes

¼ cup melted butter
Our dinner table conversations are rotting in
the fridge, somewhere between recipes that I can
never learn to replicate, and the bitter bodies of
my past attempts. When I think of you, on the
tongue of this gaping mouth of memory, you will
sit at someone else's dinner table. You will never
sit at mine

¼ cup brown sugar
The pot overflows, an angry hellfire, but
we stand cemented as conspirators. I
wonder if this is when it
ended, when we found we could
start and end this life, here,
in the kitchen.

a few inches of mom's pre-made dough
The lozenge of my heart is stuck in
your cheek, a gooey after-dinner
mint. The fridge light dims. I've tried
and failed to lay down and simmer
in your cast iron pan.

2 cups sliced strawberries
I tell you about when I knew death as little more than
being carried from the dinner table,
fast asleep in my father's arms,
his fingers wrapped around my wrist.

1 teaspoon of cinnamon
In this in-between, I hear the laughter from the kitchen,
and I wonder,
when will your recipe call for me again?

i remember lying | BEE LB

face-down. hospital bed without admission.
cold numb up and down my arm, or between
my toes, thin slice of thread through flesh.

doctor didn't know half what he was doing
left me scarred. nurses cluck and question
check my body for sign of injury. before

the bed that wasn't a bed, blood that wasn't
only blood. fat bubbling up in wound.

unless you've seen it, you don't know. i saw it
through a girl's careless tongue. didn't believe it
til i believed. had to believe once i saw.

doctor didn't have to stitch me up so rough
but he did. wore a breadbag for weeks under water.

sarah lee whitebread with the dimple across the top.
sticky and sweet clings to roof of mouth. pry it off

with wiggling tongue, swallow with mouthful of milk.
haven't had whitebread since i was little. let the bag
cling

so stitches wouldn't wet. felt a snake slither
through skin when thread pulled through. wirecutters
each snip a quick lick of pain then splinter.

don't know why i bother. decade gone, i can't remember.
but i remember lying face down. sewed up cold and numb.

blood spilling glass to floor to shattered window. held
my arm
away, as if distance could numb pain. no, i don't
remember

pain, but i know how to chase. my voice like chainsaw's
wretched groan. our ground down shocks felt each bump

in the road mom drove us down, her voice
a livewire beside me begging.

you self-medicate with cookies | Lisa Rabey

anxiety / depression / bipolar / manic / obsessive / compulsive

physically eats at you
it takes precedence
over everything
leaving you exhausted

for the singular energy you need
to generate to stay within a
range of normal that does not exist

whatever the fuck normal is

there is no control
you are a burden
(you think)
to you and everyone else
you are ashamed
you feel guilty
for being sick

it takes days to recover

this is not something you plan or even hope for
you crippled emotionally
physically
mentally
it's existential pain at its worst because
you are wondering what you did to
cause this and knowing it's nothing you have done
it just is
there should be some
blame leveled
some accusations surely

it's not your fault

you blame you because the blame
has to end with someone and

you'll take the fall as it is required

it hurts

sometimes there are no words
in my language
that articulates this pain

you could say
you see it as a pinprick of light
staring at you and
seemingly getting closer
that is your job
to outrun
outdistance
outlive
that pinprick of light
every emotion
feeling / taste / touch / smell / hear / sight
needs to be absent
from that light
so it cannot
feel you / taste you / touch you / smell you / hear you /
see you
or
acknowledge your existence

you self-medicate
you drink / drug / eat / have sex s
ometimes you think it helps
but all of the time that
self-medication is a lie

sometimes suicide seems like
the only option
the allure of peace
the one thing your brain
won't give
but even then you know
suicide is false
because the pain you
leave behind now belongs
to someone else

and the irony is as
i’m in the throes of
a manic episode
and yet i cannot tell you
what it’s like

(don't) feed the troll(s) | Stephani

you said
"we need to talk about
all these fat girls, obese girls,
acting like it's ok to be fat."

let's talk about it then.

let's talk about the time
a doctor said to me
"it's normal to gain weight with age
so i wouldn't worry about it"

like that wasn't me,
growing bigger every year
despite my best efforts

let's talk about the time
a doctor said to me
"ibs is just gas
it's not as bad as you think"

like that wasn't me,
running to the office bathroom
six to ten times every day

let's talk about the time
a doctor said to me
"you need to work out more"

like that wasn't me,
working out to the point of
damage, breaking my body

let's talk about the time
a doctor said to me
"you aren't even trying"

like that wasn't me,
devouring every book, every
thing i could find on nutrition

let's talk about the time
a doctor said to me
"it's as simple as calories in, calories out"

like that wasn't me,
keeping food journals, tracking,
meticulously counting, every last calorie

let's talk about all the times
a doctor has listened to my tears
and failed to hear anything spoken
with anything beyond suspicion and doubt

let's talk about all of the times
i have pleaded my case
only to be met with active indifference
and never once was i
offered a helping hand

let's talk about all of the people
who are chronically dismissed
by medical professionals
working within a system
more concerned about insurance billing

like we haven't been trying, trying
and trying
we're asking you to meet us
with compassion
instead of asking us to try
again

Featured Writer

Leia K. Bradley

Leia K. Bradley (they/she) is a backwoods Georgia born, Brooklyn based lesbian writer and performance artist and an MFA Poetry candidate at Columbia University, where she also was awarded the Undergraduate Writing Teaching Fellowship for 2023-24. She has work in Poetry Project, Aurore, Wrongdoing, Ghost City, Moss Puppy, Cutbow Quarterly, Versification, JMWW, Wild Greens, Trampset, Peach Fuzz, and more, with her poem "Settle(d)" chosen as the Editor's Choice Best Overall pick for Penumbra Magazine's Pride issue. After climbing out from the coffin of her first divorce, she is accepting love and lust letters through her twitter @LeiaKBradley or instagram @MadameMort.

June, Where Did You Put The Time? | Leia K. Bradley

June, It's hard to tell you just because I wrote about you
      doesn't mean I love you—in fact, it might mean the opposite—
but I let you go on believing fate is red-handed, crimson-nailed and raking
      down your back—but we won't
mention time, won't mention
      how you arrive on my doorstep at 2 AM like clock work,
double-fisting a bottle of Jack and a small Coca-Cola,
      how my mouth is a cherry I drop into your burn
to sweeten the bite of you. June,
      you twist the stems of me in your mouth,
a Celtic lover's knot, maraschino for marriage; wrapped taut 'round your finger,
      I always let you upstairs, June. Even when
I have to drink heavy, gulp quick
      to be able to swallow you down.
Tonight it's 2 AM again and I drank only
      in anticipation of your drunk. Tonight you hang me from the ceiling,
shibari chandelier,
      kiss my elbows,
balm my ropeburn with your mouth.
      I wonder when you'll realize
I'm vacant-hearted,
      fecund but foreclosed, June,
wonder when you'll notice I'm marked uninhabitable, that you're squatting
      in a molding room
built to be demolished.
      Maybe you do know
and just don't have the time
      to mind.

My frown deepens the slant and tilt of the floors. One day, June,
      we could both fall
into the apartment below.
      You've got vomit on your leather pants. You're

barely standing, so I help you undress, wash
      the acrid from your hair in the bath.
You can't stand so we lay
      on top of each other and swim like skin
could be a life raft.
      Nausea is the knowledge that you won't remember me
wrapping my arms tight around you like some sculpted pil-
lar in Rome
      while it burns itself down. Strong, palatial, June,
      you
could hold up the whole world, Atlas style,
      hunched in hubris.
But your steel gaze and steel-toed boots fail to fool
      the stagnant grief playing aubades in your middle.
      June,
I know you've lost things so dire you can't bear
      to hold them on your tongue
to flick their fleeting from your lips, to gulp down an-
other loss
      all over again. Memory's gonna kill you, June,
but you're sure giving it a leg up.

Arms behind my back, you kiss me and say I'm not allowed
      to touch you, and I obey, let you
do your worst. Gaping from lack,
      you fall on your knees minutes later
and kiss each of my thighs, your six-foot frame suddenly
too small
      to stare up, meet my gaze.
You can't even fake it, June,
      being in control. I can't even fake it—
I love you like a garden, like planting only perennials.
      Like knowing every brightest bloom,
come cold, will die.

June, if your sorrow was a building, it'd be on a hundred
acres of land.
      Madness so deep it could build its own moat.
You keep sailing and swirling
      into me, June, ceaseless as tide, as if moons and
      Manhattan
were enough to write a love story
      that doesn't end ten chapters too soon.

It's hard not to notice
you don't mind the lie of a future.
You want me to write your fate so badly,
but if I did I'd write me out of it—
you'd have a better chance at more chapters with someone
penless. Penniless I
don't know why you think
your redemption bats my eyelashes. Seven dollars in
my bra
and you know me, June, I'll buy a book
before food. We laid in bed all winter and fed each
other spoonfuls
of peanut butter, globs of
We could disappear and no one would even
come looking, come and look, it's our love
in the shape of a spider's web
in the ceiling corner. The capture and crawl, the hope-
less sprawl—
I can't wait to love you when your hair goes silver
as that silk.
But I remind you, June:
You've got to want to get to greying.

Once, you laid your your wine-dark waves on my typewriter
your curls tangling in the metal keys.
Once you wanted to be less dead, thought ink for blood
was a lover's exchange. Binging on bartered bruis
es,
now we moan on stolen time. You don't think we're meant
to live very long,
and I am porcelain with the terror
of starting to believe you.

Another night with you on my steps—
your ghosts playing in your eyes like pupils were
palms, reading
futures, reaching into an abyss
and expecting velvet—
I am no chaise longue for your pretty parlor'd rest.
June, I am all pincushion,
jabbed and jutting, more needle-sharp,
I am a thing of discomfort, disquiet, and still
you choose my doorstep. You don't remember how you got

here, you never do,
      but you remember the three trains and where to turn
to bang on my broken door.
      I picture all the boroughs strung together by cor
      set strings, subway lines
tightening in long black ribbon,
      bringing you to me blackout
but safe, always repeating my name.
      Your marble chest in a ripped shirt
spinning in your boots, beautiful as any of Saturn's re-
volving moons.
      June, you're incandescent.
In the desolate decay of January's insistent ivory sky,
      it is just another grey almost-dawn
that I helped you up the stairs and into bed.
      You thought it was yours, back home. You confused
      me for your mother.
I tuck the sheets around you like Moses
      in a basket, safely down a river
of blue sheets,
      and kiss your forehead,
and I bring a blanket to the couch. I tiptoe in
      even though you're out colder than vodka on ice in
      a chilled glass, and
put two fingers under your nose, June,
      to make sure you're still breathing
every few hours.
      And when you're gone in the morning
and back just shy of dawn, gin and vomit on your breath,
      I'll let you up again.
Your fleeting heaven, my only moon—
      I'm a Valentine past my February
but you are always June.

[end poem]

Dear Sabina Spielrein. Did You Like Being So Known?

|Leia K.Bradley

Trading traumas with a psychoanalyst
      at a Williamsburg hotel bar,
she takes me back to her office,
      fucks me on the couch.
I won't call her back. It's doomed.
      I know it can't get any more Freudian, know
after such a strong beginning
      the future could only ever echo the peak
of our Jungian, youth-scented tryst.
      No, Sabina, she is not my psychoanalyst,
but someone, soon, will
      lie on that couch to wade through their wallows
and it might still be damp from my gush.
      Laced in libidinal,
the psychoanalyst says she wants to understand
      how I can be so affable yet so impenetrable,
and I think of the deepdark place
      where secrets and desire
give themselves over to pleasure. How I'm not so sure
      she could handle that feral, ravenous need
growing roses over my headstone heart. That bloodborne,
sweet carnality
      that glows with delectable evils. When I unravel
      like that,
the moans come from somewhere else, somewhere Other,
      beneath the cavernous dredge
of all my thick facades.
      There are parts of me, these obsidian ones, that
I don't want someone gravedigging up
      to prod and poke around in. I don't think
I want to bleed myself bare
      for anyone with a magnifying glass for a mouth.
Burning
      like some ant in her searing summer.
But tonight I will follow your lead, Sabina, I will
      lay back on the psychoanalyst's couch and let her
believe
      she could tuck me neatly
into the DSM
      of her own private need.
As if my hysteria

30 was something she could dissect with her teeth,
heal
with only two scripting hands.
I don't need a savior, just the story
of how I won't bother to put her through the trying.

Mama Ain't Most | Leia K. Bradley

Most mothers don't want to know
      their daughters are smart enough to be whores.
But you know what it takes to survive in this world,
Mama.
      You told me young
it would take everything I've got, that it'd take more
than my insides,
      —all my convex, curated outsides, too.

When I came out to you, you shook your head.
      You said it wasn't the religion, that it was know
      ing
my life would be even harder
      than it inevitably,
already would be,
      that every odd was already stacking up to soar
into a sky black with vultures.

You always knew death wasn't something
      to cower beneath, that living
was the real cunt.
      You taught me love
was a chessboard, men
      the pawns
playing
      as kings, that money was the black and white of re
      ality—
you either have it, or you don't,
      and that's how you die early or die happy.

You taught me money
      was the only way to color happiness. Emerald
as summer grass. After all, you had love
      and were miserable, gemless.

I wish I could have helped that. I sure hope
      us laughing over bad men and worse sex
helped, sometimes, with that shared pain
      of endless, choiceless insistence:
you get out of bed and you just
      keep

moving
forward—

Mama I'm so tired
I ache in places I never knew were hollows.
But I look at your hands pressed to your temples, the way you catch yourself—
& put your shoulders back, clear your throat, fix your lipstick,
and I know it'd be cruel to complain
to a chin held that high in exhaustive defiance.
I know you'd say
pity
never got anything done. I know you're a battle axe
in bottle blonde.

You always said you told your father
I can't choose who I fall in love with,
and your father replied, *but you can choose whether he's gonna be rich*
or not, and you told me
your father was right. You told me
not to choose the slow death of a poor man's love,
to choose better,
be smarter. That beauty is a weapon, that the Cath olics
were right about one thing:
a body is a temple that's only holy
if you charge at the door.
Everyone is shocked you know what I do for a living
but you understand best
that the world is not built for our transcendence,
but for our subservience, our obedience, we
are not bent kneed to be mendicant, but bent-kneed
to snake our way into stealing what joys we can
while our beauty still distracts from our manicures
in their pockets, that men are the ones with money—
you just have to know how to get it out of them.

You married another poor man after my father
and you'll never let me forgive you for it.
You know it's too good of a motivator, you know
hate

is the only thing steady-handed enough
      to shake greed's beautiful, pale grip, and snap the
      bones
in several places, steady-eyed enough
      to look love in the eye and laugh
at its one dimensionality, its coward simplicity, and
      to bloody up the masquerade. A woman's body is a
      tool, is
a heart is a weapon
      is an insurance policy is rent paid is mouths fed
      is currency,
Mama,
      at sixteen I was a duffel bag of floggers,
coming home to you
      crying on the kitchen floor, again—
fucking *men*—
      Mama
if they had ever put a whip in your hand
      I wonder who you'd be now.
Mama I wonder if there's ever really a way out
      or if surviving is enough
to be able to say
      We win.
Mama thank you for teaching me that God is, of course,
real
      but he wouldn't have made money so hard to find
if he didn't want us to have to sin to be able to get it.
      You go to church every Sunday, and Wednesday night
      too,
and I imagine you in leather, laughing,
      and I want a better life for both of us, money as
      green and as simple
as summertime, want the world to
      slow down, be easy,
just for awhile,
      if not for me, then at the very least, Mama,
I want a good night's sleep for you.

[end poem]

I Am From The Planet Zablotz | Sage Tyrtle

You know that song? The one the Beach Boys sing on the radio about wishing everybody could be a California girl?

I live in California, but I'm not a very good California Girl. The Beach Boys say that, "The West coast has the sunshine, and the girls all get so tanned," but I am fatter than all the other second-grade girls. Also I have a scar on my lip and a smushy nose from being born with a cleft palate.

But you know what? Could I tell you a secret? I am an alien from the planet Zablotz. It's true! Did you ever see Zablotz? If you look at the stars, the one that's the belt of the man, it's the star right under the belt. On the planet Zablotz, no one calls anyone ugly. Also there is no broccoli. A farmer tried to grow broccoli once and his head was cut off.

Today I am at the beach with my dad's girlfriend Tamara and her daughter Summer, who is in the second grade too. Me and Summer go to the beach every Saturday. We run and run into the waves! Tamara doesn't come in the water ever because she is busy getting so tanned.

We have lived with Tamara and Summer for a long time. Daddy says we don't live with my Mama anymore because she is a Unfit Lesbian. Also cause she lives at a place called Separatist Lesbian Womyn's Land in the woods. (Everyone who lives there spells it with a y so there's no m-a-n in the word but I think that's dumb.)

I have three photos of my mama but my favourite is the one where she's in a white dress with long hair and looking out the window like she is in a fairy tale. She writes me a letter every single week! She writes me poems and tells me stories of her life in the woods. Like how one time she was watching tv and she heard a noise and she turned around and a deer was watching the tv too through the window! The most exciting animal at my life is the next door poodle who is about a thousand years old, I think.

That's how I think of her mostly. She is a Paper and Words Mama right now, and maybe someday if she stops being a Unfit Lesbian she could be a Real Mama.

On Monday me and Summer are late for schoo. We are

always late, 'cause Tamara spends a lot of time checking for wrinkles in the mirror before she drives us but today we're extra late 'cause we were up until practically midnight watching the movie *Kingdom of the Spiders* which has William Shatner in it, you know, Captain Kirk. The spiders were in people's beds under the sheets even! And the people all ran and ran from the spiders but then the spiders ate everybody anyway. I was awake forever 'cause every time I heard a sound I thought it was a tarantula coming to get me.

When Tamara drops us off at the parking lot Summer runs ahead so she can pretend she doesn't know me. She has a lot of friends, they are all named Jennifer, and the Jennifers don't like me so at school Summer doesn't like me either. (But on Saturdays. On Saturdays we stay in the water so long that our fingers turn to pruney raisins. Tamara makes us get out when our lips turn blue from how cold we are.) In class Mrs. Hoag says we have to pick partners for the volcano project and all the Jennifers run to the other side of the room like I'm gonna chain myself to them and make them be my partner or something. And they whisper-chant SA-AGE SA-AGE SHE LIVES IN A CA-AGE and I stare at my desk till Mrs. Hoag says that I will be partners with Jason and David, who only talk about soccer.

But on Saturdays. Saturdays me and Summer stand in the water which is so cold, and we wait for the next wave which is so high. And then we jump and ride the wave and if I could just ride it long enough I will make it to planet Zablotz. Where at school they always assign partners.

After Mrs. Hoag's class I sit on the soccer field. I used to go to the cafeteria during lunch, but whenever I sat at a table all the kids just got up and went to a different table. So now I go to the soccer field and eat my lunch and read Harriet the Spy. Have you read this book? Louise Fitzhugh, she is the one who wrote this book, *she is from my planet!* I know because Harriet the Spy is a bad California Girl too. She writes in her notebook all the time instead of going to the mall with Tamara and Summer. Harriet is loud! And she says whatever stuff she thinks! I was gonna write Louise Fitzhugh and ask her how to get to Zablotz but she died already.

When the last bell rings Summer goes to one of the Jennifers' houses and so when I get home I go in the backyard. I close my eyes and spread my arms wide. I pretend like I'm in the ocean and the wave that is so cold and so big crashes into me and I jump. I ride the wave and the water starts to get warmer and the sky is black. There's sparkly stars so small I could hold them. I ride the wave for so long. For so long that I make it to Zablotz. And me and Louise Fitzhugh bring our books to the park and get ice cream and it takes a long time to find a place to sit 'cause everybody there is *also* reading and eating ice cream.

My Daddy says that maybe the kids at school don't know I want to be their friend and I should have a party so they could know. He brings home a whole packet of Wonder Woman invitation cards and the next day I put one on every desk. My Daddy says that I should make A Real Effort to especially be friends with the Jennifers, so when Tallest Jennifer comes into the room I take a big big breath and stand up. I say, "I'M HAVING A PARTY," way too loud.

Tallest Jennifer just looks at me and looks at me.

My heart starts to go fast. "We'll have cake and ice cream and – there's – I have lots of Barbies –" actually Barbies are pretty boring because all you can do is take their clothes off and put their clothes on but I don't know, maybe the Jennifers like them " – you could use the Pretty in Pink Barbie, she's the –"
Tallest Jennifer says, "I'd rather *die* then go to your party."

By the end of the day there's a lot of Wonder Woman invitation cards in the garbage can. So... I don't have a party.

But on *Saturdays.* On Saturday me and Summer are getting out of the car from being at the beach and the Clarks next door are just getting home too. We run across the lawn to their driveway. Mr. Clark is getting a red cooler out of the trunk and he says, "Look what we brought home from our ski trip." And he opens the cooler and then I feel cold on my arm and I look down and it's a *snowball!* I never saw that thing before! Mrs. Clark is already making another snowball and she gives it to me and I throw it at Summer and the Clarks are laughing and it's so hot outside that the snow melts.

It melts the second it touches the driveway.

*

Okay, so you know Madonna song about being a Material Girl?

I go to the mall, like, *a lot,* but I'm not a very good Material Girl.

Because on Saturdays. On Saturdays Summer and I have ice skating lessons at the mall, because my Dad says that I need to learn, like, how to be graceful. And also stop being fat. Today after class Summer leaves with some Jennifers and I walk around the mall by myself. Right in the middle by Macy's is where everyone likes to sit around and smoke so I mostly stick to one side of the mall or the other because gross. I always stop at Crown Books and - don't tell Crown Books because they would call the police probably - but I go to the teen section and I read for free.

Right now I am reading the Sweet Valley High books. Have you read these? Jessica and Elizabeth Wakefield are *perfect* Material Girls. They are identical twins and they are blonde and a size six and mostly the books are about shopping and the boys they like. I'd totally rather read A Wrinkle in Time. Meg Murry is for sure smarter than the twins. Oh my god, Meg Murry's *dog* is smarter than the twins. But I know if I read enough of the Sweet Valley High books I'll figure out the secret of being popular like the Jennifers. The *twins,* I mean.

The first thing is to not be so fat but even then I'll still have, you know, the gross scar on my lip and my smashed in nose. Sometimes before school I look in the mirror and whisper "you are disgusting" a hundred times so I won't eat tater tots during lunch. (But then I do eat tater tots during lunch.) If I were a Material Girl I wouldn't think about Zablotz anymore. I mean, I'm fifteen. I know now my planet's too far away. If you're an alien and you can't go home you have to just, like, fit in. Be so much like them that they forget you were ever different.

When I was a little kid I totally thought that my Paper and Words Mama would write a letter one day about how she stopped being an Unfit Lesbian. Like it was the flu or something. She'd be like, "I married a man named

Greg! We have a sectional couch and a pool! I wear lipstick now! Come visit!" But she's still at the Lesbian Separatist Womyn's Land and she still has this girlfriend Daegan who actually seems really nice. Every few weeks my mom and Daegan make me cassette tapes and tell me about their life, and I make cassette tapes for them too. One time I sang the whole song "Broken Wings", I put the song in my walkman headphones so I had the lyrics, you know? And then I sang it for them.

On Saturday I'm in Crown Books reading "Bitter Rivals", Sweet Valley High number 29, it's this scene in a mall and I say, "Oh my god!" out loud and this lady in the aisle, like, stares at me but I just realized that Elizabeth and Jessica would not be seen *dead* in a JC Penney, and what am I wearing? I'm wearing Wrangler Jeans *with yellow stitching* on the sides. No wonder everyone hates me. No wonder Summer doesn't even talk to me at home anymore.

For the first time ever I ask my dad for clothes shopping money and he gives it to me. He says, "Hey, also if you lose thirty pounds I'll give you money for a haircut."

At the mall I stand in front of Supercuts and look at the hairdo pictures. Maybe when I'm not repulsive anymore I'll get a bob like Molly Ringwald. I'll be at a different Jennifer's party every night. I'll tell everyone that my *friends* call me something normal, not a weird alien name like Sage but a name like Michelle, or maybe Lisa. At lunch they'll have to drag over another table in the cafeteria because so many girls will want to sit with me!

On Monday I sit at my desk in my brand new denim jacket and put my Esprit bag on my desk. Tallest Jennifer stops at my desk. She's in Jordache jeans and a dark blue sweater that comes down to her knees practically. Oh my god. This is, like, the moment everything changes.

She says, "Wow, I guess you went shopping, huh?"

I can hardly breathe so I just nod. I am thinking that maybe I'll change my name to Jessica in honour of Sweet Valley High because she and Elizabeth are the ones who showed me how to be popular.

Tallest Jennifer says, "Um, good try." She throws her blond hair over her shoulder and smiles.

All of the Jennifers laugh and laugh and laugh.

So... I'm still really lonely.

Sometimes I go through an entire week and the only person who talks to me is my dad. Before school every day I stare in the mirror and I whisper "you should die" a hundred times. If you're an alien and no one will forget that you're an alien, and your home is too far away, then I guess all you've got are... well... I don't really know what you have.

One night my dad knocks on the door of the room I share with Summer. She's at soccer practice. I'm supposed to be doing homework but actually I'm lying on my bed watching Growing Pains (I found out in Tiger Beat that me and Kirk Cameron have *exactly* the same birthday which means we are destined to get married) and I snap it off really quick then tell my dad he can come in. I'm pretty sure he's going to ask me if I'm flunking biology.

But when my dad comes into the room he just looks at the remote control on the bed and sighs. He says after a really long time, "The school guidance counselor called me at work today." I am thinking, it's just *biology*, why does the guidance counselor care, and my dad says, "Are you... did you stop talking at school?" I just look at him. "She says it's been a month. She says she's worried about you. Really worried. Kiddo," he leans forward, "You can tell me what's going on."

He waits but I just stare at my hands. What I want to say is that I'm surprised anybody noticed I stopped talking. I want to say that sharing a room with a girl who's supposed to be my stepsister but who acts like I'm invisible makes me wonder if I exist at all. I want to say that I'm so tired of looking in the mirror and hating everything I see. But what comes out of my mouth surprises both of us. "I want to go see my mom." I totally want to take it back in the next second because *what do you talk to separatist lesbians about* but I think about my Paper and Words Mama turning into a Real Mama and I don't say anything.

My dad rubs his mouth. "Okay," he says. "Okay."
When my plane lands at the airport I'm totally scared I won't know who my mom is. I brought my picture, the one where she's in the white dress, but that was taken, like, *sixteen years ago*. I'm looking at everyone at the airport

and all the women have kids. Or are super old. Or they have husbands (named Gary probably) and so they're not her, and then I turn around – and she's not in a dress. She's in this old leather jacket. She doesn't have long hair, she has a grey crew cut. She is looking right at me and smiling and she's missing three teeth and I run into her open arms and she holds me so tight. And I don't know how I forgot this. Because the second she is holding me I remember how I have fit into her arms a thousand times before. I bury my face in her neck and breathe in the smell of sweat and cigarettes. And home.

My mom drives me from the airport in an old pick-up truck. I'm pretty quiet. I don't really know what to say. My mom's quiet too, but in a comfortable way. Like silence is okay with her. Like she'd wait for ten years if that's how long it took me to say anything.

We drive for forever. We pass a herd of horses and an abandoned farmhouse with half a collapsed roof. We drive across a creek that's so deep the water sheets up on both sides. Finally she stops the truck at the top of a steep gravel driveway lined with cedar trees. We both get out. My mom is, like, *striding.* She is barely taller than me but it's like her head is higher than the trees.

I'm trying to keep up with her but my heels keep catching in the gravel and my perm is wilted and I am pretty sure my mascara didn't survive the plane trip so great. These cicadas are screeching WEE WEE WEE and I can't even, like, think. I wish I'd never asked to come here, I wish I was back at the mall, even biology class is better than this. And then, over the cicadas, I hear women laughing.

Belly laughs, like the kind that makes your stomach hurt the next day.

I think of Tamara and how she puts her hand over her mouth when she laughs. I think of how when we were little Summer and I used to pee ourselves a little bit from laughing and how now she and the Jennifers put their hands over their mouth just like Tamara and I stop walking. I listen. I take off my heels and run to catch up with my mom.

When we get to the end of the driveway I see five women by a house sitting around a table outside, my mom tells me who they are – Judith, she's painting a picture of Wolf, who is posing for it. Happy and Owl are eating tuna fish sandwiches, and lying in the grass reading is my mom's girlfriend Daegan and when she sees me she gets up and runs over and holds my shoulders and looks me in the eye and grins. She says, "I feel like I know you from your letters." And I never thought of being the Paper and Words *Kid* but I guess I am. She hugs me and after a second I hug her back.

The one who's painting says I look so much like a woman named Turtle who used to live there and asks if she can call me Sage Turtle. I never had a nickname before. I whisper, "Yeah, that would be okay."

We sit down inside to eat BBQ tempeh and corn and pumpkin. I don't know what to say (I mean for real *what do you say to separatist lesbians*) so I listen instead. And they are talking about how the fox brought her babies to see the compost pile, and how to irrigate the gardens better which is where most of their food comes from, and Reagan's policies in the USSR. And I keep waiting and waiting but no one mentions Diet Coke. Or how much they hate themselves. Not once.

In the morning me and my mom and Daegan are eating oatmeal when Daegan is like, "Have you ever met a tarantula? 'Cause I know one and she's pretty great." And I'm really scared because I'm remembering that William Shatner movie *Kingdom of the Spiders* where the spiders eat everyone – buti if I were on Zablotz I wouldn't be scared. So I say yes.

We walk for hours. Sometimes we talk and sometimes we don't and no one ever tries to fill the silence. I watch how my mom walks through the woods like she owns them and I square my shoulders too, I look straight ahead too. It's so weird to smell trees and dirt instead of cars. When I get stuck on a steep part my mom reaches down and helps me and it feels like there are steel wires inside her arms. The trees get thinner and thinner until we're at the top of a big hill, it's all forest and farms so we can see for miles.

Daegan kneels down and moves a big flat rock that's covering most of a hole. The tarantula is the size of *a baseball* but Daegan puts her hand into the tarantula's den and it climbs right on! She looks up and smiles. "It's okay," my mom says, "you can touch her." I touch the back of the tarantula and my hand is totally shaking. I expect her to be prickly but she feels soft, she feels like a tiny cat. After awhile Daegan nudges her and she goes back into her den. Daegan pushes the rock mostly back over the hole.

We walk back and I am striding like my mom and thinking the whole time about how *I touched a tarantula.* My mom and Daegan hold hands as they walk. It's cooler on the walk back, the sun is going down and I can hear this bird going "Whipp-or-WILL! Whipp-or-WILL!" and my mom looks up into a cedar tree and points. "Hey, we're almost home."

I look up and hanging from a tree there's a big piece of falling-apart fabric with embroidery on it. There's a bunch of women in the background and then a huge bear in front of all of them, she's on her hind legs and roaring. And I don't know how the flag of Zablotz made it here. I close my eyes and for a second I am standing in the water with Summer. The wave is coming and if I can just ride it long enough...

By the third day everyone is calling me "Sage Turtle" and as a joke I start spelling it like "T-y-r-t-l-e" because I still think "womyn" is dumb but then everyone else starts spelling it that way too. For two weeks me and my mom sing and walk in the woods and weed the garden. One night I'm drifting, dozing under the covers. I can hear women's voices by the fire outside.

My mom cackles her witchy cackle. And I think of all the years that I didn't ask to see her. All the years she was my Paper and Words Mama and I just let it happen, and I feel so sad for little-kid me and everything she missed.

Me and Meg Murry rock in the hammock for hours and hours and she shows me what a wrinkle in time looks like. I walk up to the highest hill again by myself and sit sort of close to the tarantula's rock but not so close she could come out and touch me! I get out my notebook and make a list of places that aren't California. It's a really, really long list.

Now when I walk into a room someone always says "*Sage Tyrtle!*" and I like it. I like it a lot. Maybe I'll, like, use it as my pretend name when I'm grown up, like how Sting is really Gordon Sumner.

On my very last night at Lesbian Separatist Womyn's Land everyone sits around the campfire. We play gin rummy and my mom gets out her guitar and we all sing. "When I was a little girl I wished I was a boy, I tagged along behind the gang and wore my corduroys, everybody said I only did it to annoy, but I was gonna be an engineer!" As the fire burns low Owl tells a story about how her truck got stuck in the mud at the Michigan Womyn's Festival and all the women pulled her out, and then Happy talks about going to the anti-nuclear protests in St. Louis, and then my mom turns to me and says, "What's your story, Sagie?"

I look at my hands. I say, "There's a planet called Zablotz. It's the one under Orion's Belt. On Zablotz the magazines at the grocery store have photographs of famous people on the front. Like this girl, who figured out how to make clean drinking water with a really cheap filter when she was just sixteen years old. Or the old woman who overthrew an insane dictator with an army of just other old women..."

I tell them the story of Zablotz. And they are leaning forward and they are smiling and I don't even notice standing up but I do because I'm so excited and when I get to the end *they are clapping* and even though I'm still fat they are clapping and even though I'm still ugly they are clapping –

And I stand there looking at their shining faces in the firelight and – I know. I rode the wave far enough this time. I made it to Zablotz.

*

You know that song, the one by Margie Adam? The one where when she was a kid her best friend was a unicorn but now that she's grown up she's her own best friend? On Saturday I'm on the Toronto subway heading home listening to Margie on my headphones when I hear a man shouting. I take off my headphones. He hollers, "So – how are you going to defend this woman from what I'm saying?"

And in my head I'm like, "Maybe I will defend her by getting off at the next subway stop!" but my body has other ideas because I look down and I'm striding the length of the subway car. I spot him right away. He's in his thirties with wavy brown hair and a denim jacket. He's staring at a young woman sitting on the opposite side of the subway car, she is staring at the floor. Her

shoulders are hunched and though she would be tall if she stood up she's very small, sitting there.
And then the man looks up and sees me. He snarls, "You. You with the blue hair. You are the ugliest woman I've ever seen in my life!" He laughs. "The best *you* could possibly hope for is that some man thinks you are... *acceptable.*"

My hands and feet are tingling and I feel dizzy enough that I'm swaying a little. Is he really saying this to me? A complete stranger, right here on the subway car? But his words also sound so familiar. And after a moment I get it – it's like my teenage self has launched herself through space and time to posses the body of this horrible man on the subway. And I really want to say, "Oh my god, welcome to the future. I have, like, *so much to tell you.* Okay. First of all, Kirk Cameron turned out to be a fundamentalist creep, so that marriage thing wouldn't have worked out after all –"

But he's already talking again. "– and fat. You are incredibly fat. No one can stand to look at you, you ugly, fat, blue haired lesbian."

And in my head I am giggling. He is calling me warm. He is calling me kind. He is surrounding me with the people I love most in the world, laughing with wild abandon. I mean, yes, I am horrified by the great joy in his eyes as he says words he clearly thinks I will be replaying in my head for the next ten years. But he has no idea whatsoever that I made peace with my body the day I stood by the fire and told the story of Zablotz. While *Ronald Reagan* was still president.

A guy sitting nearby says, "Buddy. Time to be quiet."

And he is quiet for a little while but when it's obvious that I'm not getting off the subway he says, "Get away from me, you ugly freak! You look like a female grizzly bear!" I stare straight ahead, thinking that if I opened a coffee shop called Lesbian Grizzly Bear I would definitely make a million dollars.

I can only think of two things to say out loud. One is what my mom would have said in all sincerity: "You seem so distressed. What can I do to help?" But because I hate this man and would rather set him on fire I don't say that.

Or there's what *I* am dying to say, which is, "Sir, I was bullied in school by girls named Jennifer. I knew girls named Jennifer. Girls named Jennifer were my enemies. Sir, you could try for the rest of your whole life and you will never, ever be as scary as a thirteen-year-old girl named Jennifer."

So I simply stand there as the man thumps his chest and says, "I'm good looking. Everyone on this subway can see it, and I'm telling you, you're hideous. I should know." The subway pulls into St. George Station and the young woman gets up and leaves, and I follow her off.

That man wanted to know who was going to defend that woman. So I stood there, and silently watched, and he didn't say another word.

To her.

And I will never be a wasp-waisted plastic doll standing stiffly in the sand, arms crooked especially so I can hold some man who thinks I'm acceptable. Because I've got better things to do with my life.

You know that song? The one by the Beach Boys where they wish everyone could be a California Girl?

Here is my California Girl.

Seven years old. Sweaty and chubby and laughing so hard she is snorting. Scarred upper lip and smushy nose, throwing pieces of frozen ocean and watching them melt on the warm driveway.

So exquisitely beautiful you can hardly bear to look.

Not Much but Not Nothing |Jen Hemken

When I made an OKCupid account on my friend's recommendation, I did not expect it to send me into an existential crisis.

The app offers these personality quiz-type questions to improve your matches. The quizzes were addictive. I answered over a hundred prompts and only stopped because I realized people could see how many you did. I didn't want anyone to think I was insane.

But one question early on stopped me dead in my tracks: "How do you feel when you do nothing all day?" The options were *good* and *bad*.

I took a moment to wrap my head around the question, trying to understand what nothing even meant. When I let the days pass without doing chores, not cooking, not going out, I felt awful. I felt unproductive, useless.

But was that *nothing*?

Whenever I tried to relax, I always ended up reaching for my phone, or getting my computer, or a snack from the kitchen, watching my comfort movies or YouTube videos for the umpteenth time, always trying to satisfy some craving.

And when I thought about it, just sitting there, really sitting there without a task or goal, scared me. It reminded me of the darkest times of my depression, when I would hide in my bedroom, sometimes crawling under my bed, just staring off into space. At the time, I could go hours without moving, not watching anything, not looking at anything, in complete silence, just being alone with my thoughts. It was the worst type of *nothing*.

Therapy felt even worse than depression at first, but it started paying off after a year or so. I once had to live in a clinic for very long time. On my last day, my psychiatrist went over my medical report with me. In the summary, he had written, *the patient has major depressive disorder in remission.* "That means you are still sick, but you are not suffering significant symptoms," he said.

His voice was so practiced and hopeful. He had such a warm, honest smile. What a way to tell someone they will never be free.

For a moment, I wanted to spit on his glasses and kick his teeth in. But that is not what people do when they are in remission.

He proffered his hand, and I gave it a firm, thankful shake. I wanted to show him how healthy I was. I wanted to show it to myself.

Long before my first and worst episode, when I was still in high school, I would often just lie in my bed after lunch. Just flop down, hands behind my head, in my day clothes, on top of my giraffe-pattern bedsheets. I would just stare at the ceiling that my mother had shoddily, lovingly painted dark blue. The paint had disagreed with the polystyrene of the ceiling panels and ate into it in some places or just didn't adhere in others. The result was a vast, deep canvas of unplanned details: a cosmic ocean of darkness that flowed into lighter blues, stretching into deserts of small tears.

God, I could get lost in it. Was that doing *nothing*?

Sometimes I would look out the window, left open to let the birdsong in, or the sound of the rain, not minding that the wind swept some drops inside. My bed was so close to the window that I sometimes felt a soft mist on my face when I lay down that way.

I adored storms.

Sometimes I would masturbate, not bothering to get my laptop or my phone, sometimes not even thinking about sex. I would just touch myself, feel myself. And sometimes, I would fall asleep like that. When I woke up, I would feel disoriented, relaxed, maybe a bit angry. I would wonder if someone had come in while I slept, with my underwear around my knees and my hand between my legs. In my grogginess, I would feel embarrassed - and proud. Was that *nothing*?

I finally skipped the OKCupid question about doing nothing and shut my laptop. I opened the window a crack, sank into my beanbag chair, and tried just sitting like that. I saw the leaves of the tree outside my window sway in the wind. Did it have hundreds of leaves or thousands? I felt an impulse to google it - but I let it pass and stayed put.

I listened to the coo of the pigeons that nested in the tree. They had been there since Spring. But I only really heard them for the first time that day. I only heard them when I let myself do nothing.

Epiclesis | Nidhi Agrawal

Without Ida,
The channels of my body's Pingala lost consciousness,
The skeleton is a gravesite
Without flowers of feminine blood.
My quantum is entangled in Mother Kali's spell,
She pulls the strings of my Ida
awakens the time tides to rip off the white snowy mountains tangled in
My brain's hemispheres.
Tonight,
I invoke my Mother Kali!
This epiclesis is a confluence of
Ida and Pingala pathways,
I know,
Only when my mother will enter into
Sushumma, my life will begin.

Ref: Ida, Pingala & Nadis
Sadhguru. "The Three Fundamental Nadis - Ida, Pingala and Sushumna." Official Website of Sadhguru, Isha Foundation, Isha Foundation, 6 May 2013, isha.sadhguru.org/in/en/wisdom/article/the-three-fundamental-nadis.

with my brother | Luiza Zanardi

Alex sits across from Anne in the train. He's an awkward kid, too long and bony, and she's the opposite, with a round wholesome face and a full figure. But they have similar straight noses, pronounced chins, and eyes that shrink when they smile. Anne reads a book of contemporary high-brow women's fiction. Alex looks out the window in a mood. Anne looks up at him a few times, discreetly.

You have that look again, she says, her voice not quiet, but careful.

Alex looks at her with the eyes of a dead fish. Oh? Tell me all about it, Anne.

Anne stares back at him. It won't help you to be mad at me.

Alex looks at her a moment longer, his nose scrunched like he has something he wants to say. He turns his head back at the window and sighs. Anne looks at him for a moment longer.

She looks back down at her book. The main character in it is having an affair, which she and her college roommate always joke about when they talk about this book. Anne catches herself thinking of the reality of an affair.

The protagonist's sadness is what beguiles Anne. They seemed alike in some ways. She develops a new habit; in the margins of her copy, she writes comments, which mostly consist of poor thing or baby no. She annotates a scene featuring a bottle of wine, calling it so college. The protagonist finds that someone she disliked didn't deserve the sentiment - Anne decides to stop for now, before the pain makes her mind wander and forces her into distraction. She lets the paperback shuffle closed and pulls her legs up against her chest in the seat.Alex looks at her, unwavering. You have that look again, he says.

Anne raises her eyes to him without lifting her head, her

lips pressed to her jeans. I love you, Alex.

The ride with her brother to Berlin is long. They have to change trains in Verona. Anne has friends from there but none are in the city in the middle of the college term. Everyone was off to London, Edinburgh, Valencia, Rochester. Nevertheless, she suggests to Alex that they could take a stroll into the city to see the Old Town. He grunts in response. It's nothing exciting, he says. Alex has been in Italy - just a couple hours from Verona - for almost a year now, so he would know. Okay, Anne says, they could just find some gelato in the main station instead. She insists they get the small portions, and they sit across from each other in foldable wooden chairs, Alex's anime graphic-tee getting dirty with drops of white stracciatella. She looks at him while he lifts the wooden spoon, eating eagerly, and tries to avoid the feeling that something is off, to not think of all the skipped meals in the last times they've seen one another. She asks him a couple of questions about the city. Alex shrugs and insists he didn't think of anything as worthy of note. Not even Juliet's left boob, Anne notes.

They find their train to Munich, and board without much trouble. This time, they sit side-by-side in a lower grade train, and, after being reminded of her motion sickness, Alex lets Anne ride the window seat. Older Italian women (old Italian women, Alex would say) whose frills, puffy hair, and jewelry express their discomfort with ideas of gender stare at the two of them while they shuffle. Anne tries to make herself big in her oversized hoodie, bigger than Alex so no one will look at him ever again. As the train slowly pulls out of the station, he puts on his headphones, and doesn't say a word until they cross the border into Germany. Anne checks her phone for a text from their father, but he has only said to tell him when they were in Berlin.

When they get to Hauptbahnhof, it's night already, so there isn't much to see. Alex looks around, hands held behind his back, mouth shut, as they walk out and get on a tram. They take public transportation to her apartment, a small place in Friedrichshain. Anne puts her suitcase in her room, and sinks to the floor of her living room, back against her lowered couch.

You should go take a shower, she tells Alex. I'll get the couch ready for you.

Do I have to? he asks, scratching his head.

Yes, says Anne. She has a smile on her face. She's afraid that Alex will find it sardonic, the way she gets when she's tired. As long as you're sleeping in my living room you'll smell as nice as a bath of roses. Or at least neutral.

He mumbles something, or it might be a groan. Anne rubs her eyes. She points him to the closet where the towels are kept, and Alex takes the hint. After he is gone, Anne closes her eyes for a long moment. She meant to see her boyfriend in Berlin tonight, since she's been gone to Italy for a while to pick up Alex and tie up loose ends for her family. Now, she feels the hints of a migraine on the left side of her head. She shuts her eyes, softly at first, then harder. After five minutes of composing in her head, she sends a text saying the day has been more exhausting than she imagined, and that she misses him and hopes he has some time tomorrow.

Anne gets out the linens for Alex and considers not making his bed. Her body is heavy, but she has to wait for him to come out of the shower so she can get washed and ready for sleep. Making his bed is as good a distraction as any. Her body staggers while she does it, like she is the sheet being thrown around to fall the right way through the air. When she gets to bed, she wonders whether Alex will find the readied bed nice or passive-aggressive.

Before sleep, she texts her dad, *tucked him in. can you call me tomorrow?* To which he responds: *We'll talk in the morning.*

But the next morning, as he asks over Alex and her and the journey, he doesn't give her any answers. Their father squeezes out of her, multiple times over the next week, the promise they will both be going out of the house, doing things. They both need time in natural and cultural spaces, to relax. And he says he'll send money for this too. Anne looks down, infantilized by this. Anne takes Alex out to lunch with Noor, her boyfriend. They get along, because Noor has conversations with Alex about anime. Noor is the exception in Anne's circle, otherwise entirely queer, so he brings up homoeroticism between characters and Alex comes out of his shell. Alex is usually good at getting along with Anne's boyfriends. He's not very good at many things at the moment, but Anne is glad to see he is still good at this, a pearl of his true personality.

They eat falafel at one of the places Noor knows. Anne envies him for his knowledge of Berlin. Alex wraps the last half of his wrap in the tin foil, excuses himself to go to the bathroom, and Noor puts his shawarma down and looks at Anne. He has one of her hands in his, and moves his thumb on her palm, gently pressing. You're doing great, he says, and he means it, his dark eyes like two beads, caressing her. Anne feels it bounce off her, unable to talk herself into believing him.

I just hope he's okay, she admits. He doesn't talk to me like he used to.

Noor puts a kiss on her forehead. He seems like a good kid, and you're a good sister for it. Anne doesn't respond. Noor takes another bite of his wrap. Did you get your meds refilled? You always forget.

I'm going to, Anne replies, wishing he would ask less often, give her time to straighten it all out. My doctor wants me to start on new ones. They would make sleeping easier.

Sounds like a good thing.
Anne shrugs. She looks down at Noor's hand. His nails are kept short, although rough, and clean, his fingers elegantly ringed. Anne's own nails, limply hanging as he holds her hands, weeks old black nail polish on them.

Alex walks back outside. That was quick, Anne says.

They wouldn't let me go in the toilets, he explains, shrugging also, his thin shoulders coming close together. Anne's mouth hangs agape, and Noor starts standing up. No, it's fine, Alex says, it's fine.

Noor looks to Anne by default. It's not fine though, Alex.

No. Yeah, let's just not make a big deal of it, he says, and picks up his jacket from his seat. Can we get going though?

Yeah. Yeah, of course, let's, Anne says. They gather their things quickly, and Noor gives the men at the counter dirty eyes on the way out, saying, in his native German, they won't be coming back. A man replies in Arabic, which none of them speak.

They walk through the center of the city towards a park. Noor leaves them halfway through, to run an errand for some family member or other. Anne lets him kiss her on the cheek before going. She never admits to him that she's envious that he is from here, that he lives and breathes the city in which he was born, is a working part of it as much as it is of him. She wouldn't want to return home, but seeing family is a privilege she doesn't have in the same way he does. She glances at her phone, with a notification of incoming money on her bank account, with a text of a transfer receipt from her father. He says nothing about how to use it. Anne feels a knot in her throat.

On the other hand, Alex is right there, walking next to her. She links her arm on his.

Anne attempts to interest Alex in the Berlin landscape. On the weekend, she takes him to Mitte, close to Museum Island, through the gravel path where the Spree splits, and you can see the Bode Museum, and, further, the TV tower overlooking the city. People don't stare too much, in a way they did sometimes at home - anyone can fit into

Berlin. As days pass with minimal incident, in trains where he's not the oddest rider, where his outfits draw the least attention in the crowds, Anne feels his guard shifting, his hands falling less often in fists in his pockets. She shows him the slabs of rock and architecture. Alex looks at the big buildings. They're different from Italian buildings, he says, and Anne tells him, no shit, they're German. They're sturdy, Alex thinks, and grand, but in the classy way natural to the Germanic parts of Europe. They're controlled.

They walk through and Anne finds the Pergamon Museum. It has a lot of classical artifacts,Greco-Roman and otherwise. Alex likes the Miletan marketplace. He doesn't feel like staying there too long, his mouth a thin line, his brows weighing his eyes into apathy. Anne takes note of the art students there, as they are every time she visits the Pergamon, making studies of the pieces. She points them out to Alex. He takes a general interest in drawing, as does she. She wonders, out loud to him, what must it be like? To be that good at art, that you just hang out at a museum and draw as part of your degree.

I don't know. Must be nice to have a skill like that, he says, standing with her, glancing at them askance.

Anne chuckles. Yeah, look at us. Two mediocre suburban kids, no talents.

Maybe if we did, people might take us seriously, he says, lifting his eyebrows, and keeps walking. Anne trails after him, hands behind her back. Alex wants to be a journalist and write about entertainment and queer issues. Anne thinks it's a noble cause, she wanted to be a journalist once. She studies literature now. But she can't think of how to tell him what they had in common, what they still have.

When they're home, tired from all the walking, their dad calls. She tells him where they went, and sends him pictures she managed to get of them at the museum, some smiling. Alex refused to pose for pictures imitating statues, like when they were younger. Anne doesn't relay this. Her dad tells her, Good, I'm glad. You guys should be outside.

She's like, yeah, I know. It was a nice day I guess. Alex is less moody. Because what else can she say to him? He won't care to know it's because Anne doesn't tell him what to care about or what clothes to wear. He's a little nervous about being here with me I think. We both arc.

He got his chance to be alone in Italy. Now he needs to be somewhere with someone, Dad says. And he talks for the next minute, with Anne nodding on the other side of the line, his voice rising and rising. She never knows what to do at this point. Interrupting him might aggravate him. Not interrupting him makes her face grow red, pink. She wonders if her cheeks are inflating, her eyes growing bigger, looking younger and younger.

She lets him go on. She presses her thumb into the palm of her hand until it's over, and it's not enough to cut the thin skin there, but it leaves a purple-white mark. He has talked both of them out. And Alex is idle in her living room in Berlin, not his place in Italy, not home.

After the call, Anne reads her book before bed. The protagonist also scratches at her skin, pressing her thumbs into her forearms. Anne realizes that the antihistamines that help her sleep - one German doctor refused to give her new meds, and she still hasn't tried others, petrified they will also say no - are on Noor's bedside table.

Anne and Alex are alone in an S-Bahn car on the way back from the movie theater. There's a text on her phone. Her friends are meeting up at a park, they invite her and Alex and Noor to come along, there'll be drinks and music. Anne shows the text to Alex, who says will you get me a drink? If yes, I'll come. Anne chuckles and calls him a fiend, says she knows he's always been one anyway. There's a missed call from their dad. *we're out*, she texts him, *At this hour?*, he replies. *yeah. we're having fun.*
At the park, Anne's friend rolls a joint and they pass it

around. Anne doesn't smoke as much as she used to anymore. The shaking of her hands, her wandering eyes - she's outgrown the ease of it, how much she enjoyed being high. It used to feel like floating. The air bubbled softly like Apfelschorle. She takes two puffs - careful, not too many, under Noor's watchful eyes - and she teaches Alex how to smoke, tells him to inhale, not to worry about it. He coughs his lungs out and she smiles.

Anne leans back on her hands on the grass, watches her friends try to get to know Alex.They've formed a circle around a speaker, with a bottle propped on a phone flashlight, the light diffuse and unearthly for light. Alex is lit whitely, his nose pronounced, his freckles mixing in with the shadows. Anne wonders if this is the right move, if she should have taken him to a queer bar instead, tried to introduce him to the scene in Berlin. But Anne doesn't know that she's ready for that. Some nights, she's barely ready for her own friends. She holds onto Noor's arm so she won't lose herself in the sensation.

Occasionally she pipes up, calls Alex a weeb, a kid, and he rolls his eyes under his glasses.It's not like when he was younger, and they played cards in their living room with Anne's high school friends. She hopes he feels appropriate.

On their way back home they half-stumble in chilly night air. Noor makes fun of Anne, how she's drunk on so little, and Alex laughs, a full belly laugh. Anne knows she is drunk because she puts her elbows on her knees and her face on her hands, and tells Alex how much she loves him, and how glad she is to be able to hang out with him.

She texts her dad, *can you tell me what you wanted to talk about?* He doesn't answer. She thinks he'll call her in the morning. He will ask if she's taking her meds. That night, she washes her face, swallows a pill meant for something other than sleep, and waits for the side-effect to come awake in Noor's arms.

The last of April and May have zoomed and dragged by in turns. It's a rare sunny day in Berlin. Alex is on an afternoon date and Anne is cleaning the house, glad to have time to do things with the school break having finally started. She sees small spots of blood on his towel, and on his sheets. She asks him if he's on his period, and Alex says no. They have a conversation about IUDs, and not having periods, and Anne says that when they go back home he can maybe get some form of contraception that will stop his period. It helps some people with dysphoria, she says, and Alex nods.

Anne realizes Alex's showers are much quieter now than when he was in his younger teens.They used to tease him when he belted in the bathroom songs that were young like him,giving the whole house a concert. She comes into the living room while the water is on, and on the floor, just under the arm of the couch, is a torn apart razor, with a blade missing. Anne tries to put it back in place, just as she found it, quickly, her hands shaking. Then, she changes her mind and takes it away, brings it into her room. She throws it into a drawer, where her bandages are stored, and throws herself into bed. It's a soft pillow, a soft mattress. Her face is so sunken into the pillow that her tears warm up her cheek.

Anne stops reading her book. She thinks it's because she can't handle the fact that the protagonist wants to kill herself. Anne is bothered by suicide. She imagines, accidentally, slitting her throat, and she doesn't want to be there, but now that she's here, how can she get out? The character whose husband cheated on her in the book writes a three-four page long email to the protagonist. She loves the book, but she won't read it for now. This is one of the few things she thinks of to make her more stable, but it leaves her in the idleness of not having a book to read.

She decides with the help of a friend she needs to confront her father about Alex's situation. He can't possibly stay there for much longer. She doesn't know what to do, and he should have been in therapeutic care all these years, she's just his sister. She's just his sister. She says she'll do it tomorrow, on a sunny late May afternoon, and Noor hugs her, kisses her, says she can do it.

Wishes her luck.

But her father prompts it out first. He's finished school now, he says, so he doesn't need to be anywhere. We thought he could stay with you a little longer and study for the Maturitá.

Over the summer, of course, but also next semester. Anne is silent for a moment. This starts her father on the practical matters related to Alex staying in Berlin, such as studying German and having a social circle, and of ways they could remedy that, and the money he and mom will send. Bureaucracy with which Anne has to deal. Their dad doesn't say it, but he would have them both fly home for the semester if he knew of Anne's own concerns. That's where he thinks they should be. In a place where the only option is for everything to be fine.

I don't think this is such a good idea, says Alex later, stirring his cutlery around his plate instead of eating. I don't know why you would even agree to it.

Don't be an ass, Anne says, though she can't find a bite to put in her tone.

What, 'cause you're afraid to? He asks. Anne looks up at him. He doesn't snap out of his disinterest, but he does look at her from under his thick brows.

You have to be somewhere with someone, Alex.

He chuckles through his nose. You sound like Dad.

Anne breathes in slowly. There's a lilt halfway through it, a break. That's hurtful. I'm just trying to help.

Alex narrows his eyes, accusatorily, sharpening the apathy out of them. Anne had imagined this look on his face a thousand times. You're not being fair to me. You're too busy feeling bad for yourself. Go touch some grass, Anne.

Anne's eyes are stinging as she stands up. And when are you fair to me? You're eighteen, I get it, it's a horriible age to be. But I don't know what you expect me to do when I find your razor destroyed on the floor.

Alex is silent for a moment. He looks up at Anne, his mouth agape. She's run out of breath, she realizes. Alex looks shell shocked.

I knew you took them, he says, in a whisper. Alex looks down. I wish you could be on my side, he says, and Anne tells him she is, she is, he's living with her, of course she is. He looks at her. Anne watches as his eyes soften, drift away, to the place only he can inhabit and know. Anne has thought for years now, if only she can see it, they can grab what he needs, and she can pull him out. She was a fool to think he might come out intact.

Anne leaves her seat. She goes around the table, and kneels next to him. Alex. Alex, look at me, she says, and she shakes him by the arm until he's forced to. I can't let you hurt yourself.

Alex looks down at Anne. He swallows. He is so thin now, his Adam's apple juts out. His eyes brim behind his lenses, like they did years ago, when Anne trailed after him in retreat from fight with their parents. Alex resisted, but Anne wanted to know why he was so mad, so bothered, by their father's asking him to take off his sweater, why he couldn't just do it; until he told her he wasn't a girl.

I just want the pain to be gone, Anne, I don't know where to put it, he says.

I know, she says, holding his hand. Anne purses her lips. She circles her thumb on his hand, softly. I'm so sorry.

And Alex looks at her, his brows knit together, his eyes big. It's hard for Anne to picture her own face, but her heart breaks at the notion that this, too, is how she looks in pain. He slides to the ground, slotted between her and furniture, and hugs her. Anne runs her fingers through his hair, straight and soft like her own.

tonight I watched a luna moth emerge | Logan Elizabeth Craig

tonight I watched a luna moth emerge
from her cocoon her whole body
an achy joint I felt each thread-legged
step to the flatbed of a philodendron
leaf and waited for a honeyed hour
as her wings unfurled into paper-thin
velvet and how it must have hurt how
I must have forgotten how it felt to grow
my own bones to know that marrow-deep
pain could promise something good.

St. Joseph, Patron Saint of Death | Logan Elizabeth Craig

You settle in the swing beside me
on St. Joseph's beach. Cardboard sandals
hang off our wrists and I clutch
a 24-ounce lemonade in my small hands
as our feet brush through sand
glittering like ice. You say,

my neighbor takes experimental drugs
to kill the bugs beneath her skin,
to crush their one million legs and
help her sleep. The lemonade stings
sweet on the back of my throat.
I say, we should walk to the lighthouse.

It's 64 degrees in July. Life is tenuous,
I say, and the lakes freeze over so thick
you could drive across to Mackinac.
Everyone knows that, you say. Your hands
crystallize in the wind and blow away.

Did you know that when your mother dies, you live
to see if you'll make it that long, I say,
but some kids scream over my voice and jump
into the waves of Lake Michigan, shrill
and shivering. I wonder if I'll die in 2043.

No One Tells You About Before

How you'll thread headstones with Hector, who will highlight the frequency of grass trimming and inquire what features your father is looking for, as though you're pricing real estate, comparing retirement plans, or considering travel routes ahead of a long journey. Which, I suppose, you are.

"Maybe a tree," you'll stammer, thinking of your father's fondness for summer breezes, for oxygen, and shade.

You'll select a plot sized for one; your mother has refused to be buried beside him. Later, you'll realize the mistake. You should have purchased just-in-case space for two, in the event she changed her vengeful mind.

But then you would not have been near the tree.

No One Tells You About Before

How the doctors will tell you it's terminal and there's nothing they can do, but then they'll present options anyway: experimental drugs, electrodes, knives-none of them remedies but all of them cures for the pain you feel today. You'll choose cruelties that masquerade as hope to steal one more birthday, one Christmas, one spring.

You'll grasp your father's still-strong hand while the poison drips in and swaddle his concave shoulders with oven-warmed blankets, a futile attempt to ward off the encroaching, inevitable cold.

"Get your affairs in order," they'll say, but nobody quite knows what that means. Affairs suggests lovers, conquests, trysts, except that chapter's long gone, if ever it was written at all. You'll make an appointment with a lawyer and that purple-suited guy at the bank. You'll write a will, grateful, for once, for Dad's lack of awareness about how little he has to leave. You won't ask about the key for the safety deposit box that will later turn out to be empty, that Dad's been paying on for years. You won't think to amass passwords: for his computer, the cable company, or the website for the educators' pension.

In the end, you'll leave many affairs out of order.

No One Tells You About Before

How the Hospice lady with the mouse-brown hair will teach you to administer morphine, and how to manage Dad's pain, but not your own. She'll caution that his breath will become ragged but won't warn how your own breath won't come at all.

No One Tells You About After

How you'll tear a scream through the night when he leaves.

How his long-closed eyes will open azure and gaze with love and longing upon something or somewhere or someone that is not you.

No one tells you about After.

How your mother who'd distanced herself from his sour-breathed illness will crawl into your dead father's lap and ask you to take a photograph, their last as a couple. You'll do it, of course. You have a phone and thumbs. But no sense. She'll never be able to look at that picture, and you'll never be able not to.

No one tells you about After.

How in grief there are responsibilities. The lists, the calls, and dread. How the medications must be disposed of immediately. How we'll dissolve tablets into hot water and pour the red tincture over rice. A cocktail no one will be permitted to drink.

And no one tells you about After.

How you'll call the one number they gave you that day, and like a scene stolen from Shakespeare, two men in smoke-blackened jackets will knock three times on the door.

How you'll drag aside a knock-kneed table to make room for the gurney and bag.

How you'll suggest his favorite pajamas, so he won't catch cold.

How you'll never see them close his eyes.

How you never thought about afterwards before.

Biographies

(in order of appearance)

Michele Rule is a disabled writer from Kelowna BC. She is especially interested in the topics of chronic illness, relationships and nature. Michele is published in *Pine Cone Review*, *Five Minute Lit*, *Spillwords*, *WordCityLit*, *Okay Donkey*, and the anthologies *F*ck the Patriarchy*, *Chicken Soup for the Soul*, and *To Live Here*, among others. She is an associate member of the League of Canadian Poets. Michele's first chapbook is Around the World in Fifteen Haiku. Michele lives in a beautiful garden surrounded by people who love her just the way she is. Find out more about Michele at www.linktr.ee/michelerule.

Amani-Nzinga Jabbar is an African-American Muslim woman. She is a teacher, writer, and public speaker. Amani-Nzinga holds both an BA and an MA in English Literature & is currently pursuing an MFA in Creative Writing. Her work has appeared in publications such as *midnight & indigo*, *Halal Consumer Magazine*, *Muslim Girl*, *HerSTRY*, and *MALA National*. Her personal narratives, creative non-fiction essays, and fiction stories currently focus on helping other women find strength in the midst of struggle. Her novel, *I Bear Witness*, was published in April 2020 which was awarded the Daybreak Press Book Award. Her follow up novel, *Sadiya's Story*, was published in fall of 2022.

Laura Mills (she/her) is an academic in the University of St Andrews School of International Relations. Her creative work has received multiple awards, with her poetry appearing in publications such as *Survive and Thrive* and being featured as best practice in the *Gregynog Ideas Lab*. Originally from Northern Ireland, she now lives in Scotland.

Tatiana Shpakow is an anthropology student from

Albuquerque, New Mexico, currently attending Kenyon College in Ohio. Her work discusses the navigation of heteronormativity in love, the struggle to find identity as Queer, mental health, and the social sciences. Her creative work has appeared or is forthcoming in *HIKA*, *the interlochen review*, and elsewhere. She has also received the 2020 Michigan State New York Life Award from the Scholastic Art & Writing Awards.

BEE LB is an array of letters, bound to impulse; a writer creating delicate connections. they have called any number of places home; currently, a single yellow wall in Michigan. they have been published in *FOLIO*, *Figure 1*, and *The Offing*, among others. they are a poetry reader for Capsule Stories. their portfolio can be found at twinbrights.carrd.co

Lisa Rabey (she/they) contains multitudes and makes a delightful companion to trivia teams. Lisa watches a lot of reality and period television as well as reads heaving bosom books. She writes a GenXer about town newsletter at https://amostunreliablenarrator.substack.com/. Her favorite Elizabeth Bennet is Keira Knightley. She is @heroineinabook.

Stephani is an artist, writer, and chronic idealist. She has studied art at Cornish College of the Arts and Central Saint Martins. She earned a Bachelor of Arts in Humanities from Washington State University, where she received awards for her writing and graduated with honors.

Leia K. Bradley (they/she) is a backwoods Georgia born, Brooklyn based lesbian writer and performance artist, editor at *Moot Point Magazine*, and an MFA Poetry candidate at Columbia University, where she also was awarded the Undergraduate Writing Teaching Fellowship for 2023-24. She has work in *Poetry Project*, *Aurore*, *Wrongdoing Magazine*, *Ghost City Press*, *Tarot Literary*, *Versification*, and more, with her poem "Settle(d)" chosen as the Editor's Choice Best Overall pick for *Penumbra Magazine*'s 2022 Pride issue. She can be found dancing through candlelit speakeasies or climbing barefoot up a magnolia t tree with a tattered copy of *Stone Butch Blues* tucked into her dress. After climbing out from the coffin of her first divorce, she is accepting love and lust letters through her twitter @LeiaKBradley.

Sage Tyrtle's work is available in *New Delta Review, The Offing, Lunch Ticket*, and *Apex* among others. She is the author of the novella *The King of Elkport*. Her words have been featured on NPR, CBC, and PBS.Read more at www.tyrtle.com.

Jen Hemken wonders if they're a Berliner yet, having lived in the city for three years. They love to nerd out about neurotransmitters, but with their writing they try to capture the ordinary. They have a master's degree in English and almost became a journalist.

Nidhi Agrawal, who grew up in India, focuses on issues of emotional and physical trauma in her poetry. She strongly believes that poetry is a source of joy, pain, and wonder; a tool that keeps her going in life, and is driven by the intense physical and emotional trauma she encountered through her medical condition. Her writings have been featured by *Laurel Review, Altadena Libraries, Project Muse* sponsored by John Hopkins University, *Hobart Books, Quadrant Australia, Xavier Review Press, California State Poetry Society, Chronogram Magazine, Letters* (Yale University), *Setu Journal, South Asian Today, Indian Periodical, Garland Magazine, Muse India*, and many more. She is the author of 'Confluence' and an esteemed contributor to the 'Suicide Volume 2 Poetry Collection'.

Luiza Zanardi is a Brazilian creator based in Berlin, Germany. She has studied in various international institutions and is finishing a degree in Literature & the Humanities in Winter 2024, where she has studied under authors such as Clare Wigfall and Rebecca Rukeyser. She speaks rather loudly and is generally happy about being a passionate person - which she hopes shows in her fiction.

Logan Elizabeth Craig (she/they) is a future therapist training in Chattanooga, TN. Most of her poetry can be found in screenshots she's sent in her friends' group chats, but a few can also be found in *miniskirt mag*, *the lickety~split*, and *Sonder Travel Magazine*. Find them occasionally on instagram and twitter: @loganelizabethc.

Annmarie Kelly is the host of *Wild Precious Life*, a literary podcast about making the most of the time we have. She loves kickboxing, karaoke, dogs, ping-pong, books that make her laugh, movies that make her cry, and salads other people make her eat. She lives in Cleveland, Ohio, with a black and tan puppy named Archibald.

Thank You to Our Supporters!

Mounmo Bayangmbe | Zeljko Stanojevic | Oumou Aidara | Naomi Sparks | Rachel Anand | Anne-Cécile Picardo | Maria Putignano | Noahphin | CarrieAnne Winter | Joanna Wilbert | The Creative Fund by BackerKit | Jan Ringwald | Yepez Family | Will Spohn | Jean Gregory | Laura Yepez | Kathleen Vigil | Anthony Vigil | Mitchell Roe | Finn Burnett | Irma Yepez Klassen | Maggie Russon | Martina Kitty Barnes | Nelson Cooper | Rob Yepez | Alice Mrongovius | Katherine Jennifer Hemken | Irma Yepez | Lily | Erin Abbott-Haines | Erin Macnair | Michele Rule | Katie Kay | Tatiana Tomljanovic | Marie Beswick Arthur | Marion Lougheed | Asakuno | chesscommands

Milton Keynes UK
Ingram Content Group UK Ltd.
UKHW020627041223
433748UK00012B/59

9 783000 774218